the lagom book

A Balanced and Happy Life from Sweden

Linda Davidsson

contents

introduction

Congratulations on purchasing *The Lagom Book,* and thank you for doing so.

The following chapters will discuss what lagom is and how you can bring this Swedish practice into your home. Much hygge is to the Danish people, lagom is a way of living for the Swedish people. There are quite a few differences between the two practices, but you may also notice some similarities.

To start off with, we will begin by going over how to bring lagom into your life. This will give you a rundown of what this is and will show you how you can use it in your everyday life, as well as your work life.

Then we will go into how lagom can affect your family. A lot of people parent with lagom in mind, and they use it in their relationships. It can make a huge difference in the dynamics of these relationships and brings about stronger connections with those you love.

After that, we will look at how to use lagom with food. Lagom isn't a diet by any means, but it does give you some helpful practices for looking at food differently. It could change your entire eating habits.

Then, we'll go into the style of lagom. Much like hygge, you can use lagom to help choose your clothing and the design of your house to help express your way of lagom life.

Lastly, we will look at how lagom can make the world a better place. Since it focuses on the idea of less, it can help to lower your footprint and make the world a healthier place to live for everybody.

There are plenty of books on this subject on the market; thanks again for choosing this one! Every effort was made to ensure it was full of as much useful information as possible. Please enjoy!

one
bringing lagom
to life

LAGOM, pronounced law-gohm, is much more than just a funny-sounding word. What does it mean? Lagom is a Swedish philosophy that can be translated to mean "not too much, not too little." Most people will describe lagom as a concept for finding balance.

This Swedish way of life boosts the idea of keeping just the things that you absolutely need and nothing more. This is just yet another reason to love Sweden. To the countries amazing food and views, it's easy to understand why people love this place. In recent years, there have been other parts of the world that have started to pull parts of this Swedish living into their life and routine.

After all, wouldn't it be right to learn how to live in one of the happiest countries in the world?

Lagom might just be one of the aspects of Swedish culture that helps to make the country and its people so happy. That's why I believe it's important to learn a little bit about what lagom really is. The following is what you need to know about this lifestyle to help bring it into your life.

A Swedish Way of Living

The majority of us know that Swedes tend to be minimalists. This idea that we need to be more appreciative of the things that we have is not new to us. Minimalism is something that people have started to take more seriously.

This is especially true when it comes to the new ways we have started to reduce the amount of waste we create. Lagom helps to build upon this idea of minimalism and new ways to find joy in the things we own. If you would like to bring a bit of Swedish life into your home, then lagom would be a great place to start.

When it comes to the art of "balanced living," you have to take a look at the things you have in your life and figure out what it is that you absolutely need. Lagom doesn't mean that you have to get rid of everything you own, but you do have to reduce the amount of clutter that you have that is taking all of your attention and time. How does one live lagom? I'm glad you asked because there isn't a one-size-fits-all approach here.

The idea behind this is that you can improve your life by getting rid of the things that are creating stress and helping bring you more happiness. Lagom teaches us that everything in life has a natural balance. Once we figure out how to walk the line between not too little and not too much, we can find what it means to be content.

·   ·   ·

In recent years, people in America have started to jump on the lagom bandwagon, but why. If you look at how crazy life has become in general, it all makes sense. We are craving a world of balance and tranquility. Mindfulness brings us to the KonMari cleaning method, which takes us to use hygge to design our homes, which leads to lagom. All of this is in an effort to bring more balance into the places of our lives that need it.

Lagom works on an individual level. What might work for one person may not be right for another. It can also work on a larger scale as well, where the world is an amount that is seen as just and fair. In fact, in Swedish culture, it is believed that the world was started as a way to describe the right amount of things when it came to fairness. Think about a bunch of Vikings at sea, thirsty for something to drink. They have only one mug to share amongst themselves, so they have to make the beer in that mug last "all around the team."

If each one of the Vikings were to drink just the right amount, everybody in the group would get some, and everybody would be content. Doing so would not only be fair, but it also ensured that everybody had a fair chance of survival.

Then we jump forward about a thousand years, and lagom can be seen as the symbol for much more than just what is fair. Lagom is sometimes seen as perfection; just think about Goldilocks and her "just right" porridge. It helps to describe a relaxed and tranquil state.

If you were to ask a Swede how their day was, you'd hope they would say that it was 'lagom' busy. That means that there was just enough time for them to stop at the water cooler and chat without looking like they needed to be somewhere else. It seems as though the Swedes have become so good at adhering to a lagom lifestyle that they have taken it to extremes as well. Swedes are lagom intrusive, lagom loud, and lagom friendly. This is all based on standards that were developed over several generations. Many people believe that this way of life was started because of the crazy cold winters.

The Long, Cold Winters

Before the creation of central heating, multi-generational families would have to congregate in small quarters close to their heating source. This meant that if anybody had any sort of disagreement with another person, they would have to work through it in front of a large group. To keep some semblance of peace in the group, Swedes got really good at shaving of eccentricities.

The need for them to behave and conform discretely to benefit the entire group is still seen today. You get on a packed Stockholm subway during December, you will get to see lagom firsthand.

You will enter into a sea of black clothing. Swedes tend to dress alike due to their eagerness to adhere to this idea of not too much and not too little, and perhaps to create some anonymity. Who was the one who decided to create this monochromatic dress code and sent out the color matching memo?

Having just the right amount of bright colors would do the soul well during the time of year when they are enveloped by total darkness. Instead, this need to conform to others tends to override their want for self-expression. For the Swedes, fitting in assures them that they are living lagom.

So, why do American's want to adopt this idea of lagom? In America, we have been taught to push boundaries and reach for the stars. If good is good, then more has to be better.

That's not how the Swedes see it. For Swedes, the perfect state is reached once the brakes are pressed just at the right moment. Lagom lives within the middle of overindulgence and deprivation. It simply makes sense.

The first cup of coffee that you have each morning could be a special treat. However, that's not the case when you know there are four more to come. That very first piece of chocolate is delicious, but the tenth feels like guilt.

The Vikings wouldn't have survived if they had that mindset. If only one or two of them drank all the beer, the rest of them would have become dehydrated, and most of the crew would have likely died. While the American way of living has brought about a number of amazing things, it also serves as a reminder that just because you can do something doesn't mean you should.

Deep inside our minds, I feel we all know this. That's why many of us want to learn and live the lagom way. We want to find more balance in our lives. Sure, Swedes do get impressed by money, but when it is displayed in a lagom manner. They aren't for our exaggerated displays of material belongings.

Swedish Living

If you would like to learn how to live a Swedish life, finding balance is only one part of it all. Swedish living is unique due to the variety of traditions and practices that help to make life a little bit better. Lagom is all about:

- Exercise
- Being sustainable
- Living in harmony
- Seizing the positive in each moment
- Balance
- A way to deal with routine

For example, a lot of Swedes like to use capsule wardrobes to help lower their stress by ensuring they always have different articles of clothing that can be worn together. Since the capsule wardrobe helps to simplify the outfit picking process, they don't have to spend as much time and effort on getting dressed, doing the laundry, or going shopping.

There are other things that also embody this idea:

- Balanced eating

There is no need to go all-or-nothing with each meal that you have. Eating what you need, whether it be something healthy, unhealthy, sweet, or wholesome, is perfectly fine. Sustainability plays a major role in lagom, so try planning out your meals ahead of time and buy just what you need.

. . .

Once excessive products have been cleaned from your home, try to avoid purchasing things that you don't absolutely need. There is a chapter later in this book that will really look at the connection between lagom and food.

- Taking breaks

The Swedish people are big believers in the power of balanced energy. One thing you can practice is called Fika. Fika, pronounced Fee-ka, means that you take a break for cake and coffee, where you get to spend some social time with the ones you live with.

If you ever searched "what is the Swedish equivalent of hygge?" then the word lagom most likely popped up. Lagom and hygge are similar in that it's all about making your life happier and more comfortable. Even breaks you take by yourself where you prop your feet up and relax for a bit can be beneficial.

- Remove the drama

To achieve a lagom life would mean learning how to remove the things in your life that you don't need. There is a lot more to it than simply removing the clutter from your home. You also have to take a look at your life and think about where you may be accumulating too much stress.

What areas are starting to weigh you down emotionally? Do you spend too much of your time at work, and not enough of your time is spent with people you love? Do you let yourself get too involved in drama that doesn't provide you with any value?

- Be positive

This plays off of the last tip. The idea behind lagom is being in opposition to excess, which is why their goal is to find balance. Finding "enough" is their ultimate goal. This dispels the idea that being satisfied in your life is a bad thing. We don't have to constantly strive towards something new or different. We can be happy with our lives as they are. This all goes into being able to find the positive in every situation you find yourself in. You can learn from every experience you have and aspire to live in harmony with the world.

Basically, if you can find happiness even in some of the darkest places in life, this will help you to live a more lagom life. In fact, doing so is essential in the craziness of the world.

- Remove excess stuff

A cluttered home will only create a cluttered mind. This is a big part of lagom. After you have started to get rid of the emotional mess in your life, try to focus on the physical items you own. Work through your house, room by room, and figure out if you actually need everything you own. You will have to be ruthless with yourself. The more that you can throw out, the more freedom you will start to have.

- Be conscious about your purchases

Nowadays, most of us will buy things on autopilot and not think much about the process. When it comes to online shopping, it makes it way too easy to buy too much. Lagom wants you to be more present when you start to bring new things into your life.

- Exercise and sleep

While lagom is very much an inner state, its philosophy is made up of many concrete applications. Remember, it's all about balance, and that means finding time for rest and exercise. Both of these things help to clear the mind and help you to deal with life. Finding time to relax and indulge in things you enjoy is a way to recharge from the worries and anxiety of life. Lagom is big on the idea of "rituals." These are simple activities that we dedicate to ourselves to help us find our deepest needs and live more consciously.

- The environment and sustainability

A big part of the lagom philosophy is knowing the importance of recycling. This not only includes knowing how to reuse and give new life to old items but to moving old things and furniture around with taste, creativity, and imagination. Everything about lagom is based on energy saving, sustainability, and respecting the environment.

- Simple and functional

Lagom is all about versatility, utility, moderation, and harmony. All of these things can be applied to your home, so that's why lagom teaches you to choose functional and logical furniture. Ikea, a well-known Swedish furniture company, has an entire line of furniture that keeps lagom at the forefront of its design.

. . .

There are also some rules when it comes to organizing your home, as well. First off, put all of the desks or reading corners where you do most of your work close to windows. This will help you to take advantage of natural lighting and will save on electricity. You should also think about using wood for furniture and coverings because not only is it warm, but when processed, it doesn't release as many pollutants. When it comes to blankets and cushions, they like handmade materials like cotton and wool. They also tend to go for neutral colors like grey and beige. This helps create warmth in the house.

You'll also see a lot of plants in a lagom house. Plants help remove pollutants from the air, and it creates small areas of peace within the home. Having plants that you can cook with is also very lagom, as is having a garden. It's all about sustainability and making life easier.

A lagom house will be welcoming and comfortable, but it is also sustainable and ecological.

- Imperfection is beautiful

A big part of lagom is to move away from the unattainable goal of perfection. There isn't anything in life that is more frustrating than trying to attain perfection. Wonder is found within the middle ground. It is within the moments of imperfection and imprecision. After we have figured out what balance means to us, then it is up to us to defend that space by taking small action steps. To find true happiness means you know how to immerse yourself in your life's joy.

Bringing Lagom Into Your Life

Besides the few tips we have just gone over, there are a couple of other ways to bring lagom into your home. Lagom is very much a frame of mind. If you plan on living a balanced life, you will have to become more mindful of it each day.

When it comes to lagom, you don't have to go out and spend money as soon as it comes to you to get the first new products. Lagom wants you to save your money so that you can spend it at the right time.

This helps to make things easier for you when it comes to deciding on what you really want while also helping you discover that balance between financial preparation and indulgence.

Lagom wants you to take a look at your work-life balance as well.

All through history, Sweden has been connected with happiness and having a good quality of life. A big reason for this is how they approach work. While the Swedish people are committed to working hard and doing it well, they are also big on taking breaks.

Fika breaks, which I mentioned earlier, are a big part of workplaces in Sweden. It's also extremely rare for them to have to work overtime. You have to ask yourself if you are bringing balance between your work and personal life, or are you placing too much on your plate in a certain area of your life? Keeping a balance between work and life is also important when studying.

. . .

Allowing yourself to become lost in academics is just as stressful as over-committing to work.

The Curious First Step

We've gone over what lagom is and tips for living lagom, but I feel we can break that down into more actionable steps. Curiosity, to me, is a great way to look at lagom. Take, for example, the idea of Goldilocks' and how she was curious and experimented with things. We need to take that and apply it to our lives and see what areas we can make changes to.

- Stuff: We probably all struggle with owning too much stuff. I've downsized quite a few things in my house like clothes, shoes, and toys. Lagom really embraces the idea of not consuming too much and trying to make choices that are more environmentally friendly. Consider these questions:
- What areas of your home do you have too much stuff? What is one room or area that just feels overstuffed that you could declutter?
- What is something that you could do to live more sustainably? Here are some ideas:
- Shop at consignment stores and thrift shops
- Pass down things and accept hand-me-downs
- Bring reusable grocery bags to the shop
- Use refillable water bottles
- Use a coffee mug instead of disposable cups
- Screen time: This is a big area of concern for many families. It has been reported by the American Academy of Pediatrics that children spend about seven hours each day in front of the screen. Seven hours is a bit too much screen time for children. The average adult consumes about ten hours of

screen time each day. Here are some ways to battle this:

- Start tracking your and your child's screen time to get a more accurate picture of how much your use your screens.
- How can you lower the amount of time you spend on these screens by just an hour a day?
- Activities: Are you or your child taking part in too many activities? Do you spend most of your day driving to multiple appointments? One way to fix this problem is to allow one activity per child each season outside of the time they spend at school. This may not work for every family, so you have to start out by answering some questions and evaluating your situation.
- Do you feel harried by the number of activities you or your family takes part in? If not, then this isn't something you really need to think about.
- If you do feel this way, then write down all of the activities. Does every single one of them deserve a space on your calendar? What could you cut to get it down to a just-right amount?
- Time outside: Since we spend most of our time looking at screens, we probably aren't getting outside enough. Here are some ways to get more outside time:
- Plan one outside activity each weekend, at the very least.
- Plan a short walk outside each day.
- Sleep: How much sleep do you get each night? The average adult is supposed to get seven hours asleep at night, at least. Figure out what you are currently getting, and then set a goal to improve your sleep.
- Start tracking your sleep if you aren't sure how much sleep you have been getting.

- Set a bedtime for yourself to ensure you get your ideal amount, and try to turn off all screens about an hour before that.
- Gratitude: Practicing gratitude has a number of benefits, and it isn't something that is all that complicated to practice in the first place. All you have to do is write down three things you are grateful for every day.

Lagom is all about finding that just the right amount for you, so keep that in mind when going over these things.

Working the Lagom Way

First and foremost, this means that you keep a good work-life balance. Working people are human beings, not machines. We all have complex lives and relationships. While work may be important, rewarding, and at times, fun, it shouldn't be the one thing that takes up our life.

The Scandinavian HR model takes a humanistic, holistic approach to work. It has a multidimensional attitude towards work in relation to societal and personal wellbeing. This is something that many of us want in our life. It is also a great example of how a collaborative culture and individual empowerment can work well together. Scandinavians value individual responsibility, and most of their companies will work in a non-bureaucratic way with shared accountability and responsibility.

What really sets them apart from how the rest of the world works is their emphasis on employee wellbeing. While employee happiness is just now becoming thin in the West, Scandinavia has long been placing emphasis on the importance of these qualities in working life.

Lagom at work translates to Scandinavians having one of the shortest work weeks. They get paid holidays and leave, and they often get a year of parental leave. 25% of employees get to choose what their working hours are. The Swedish government has even started to look at making their work days only six hours long.

Unfortunately, we can't force businesses to change the way they work in the rest of the world. There are some who are starting to put their employee's needs first, but for the majority, it's still focused on the money they make. That means it's up to you to find your balance where you can.

For some, this could mean accepting the fact that they need to quit their job and find one that is more work-life balanced. For others, you may just need to speak with your boss about reducing your hours each week to allow you a better life.

Finding What Lagom Means to You

Like a lot of areas of the Scandinavian culture, getting the most out of lagom also involves learning what works well for you. I can go over the history of lagom for you, but in the end, it's up to you to discover your own balance in the world.

Oftentimes, the best way to bring lagom into your life is to look at the universal balance. This means that if you would like to encourage the world to send you good things, you have to give the world something good. Random acts of kindness and being good-natured are normal things for the Swedish people.

When you are a part of a community that places kindness first, it is reasonable to expect that you will get some type of care in return once you need it. It's also important to remember that balance will have ebbs and flows. You will find times when things start to feel as if they are out of balance. For example, if you have a test coming up, then you might have to spend extra time studying. If you want to get a promotion at work, then you may have to spend a bit more time at work.

The main thing with lagom is to remember not to let the imbalance go on for too long. When you allow yourself to recognize the areas of your life that are off-kilter, you will know how to bring yourself back into balance.

two
lagom and family

IF YOU'VE BEEN PAYING attention to world cultures, you probably have noticed the concept of hygge. This is the Danish way of finding contentment and coziness. This concept caused many stores to sell out of cozy socks, fuzzy sweaters, hot beverages, candles, and whatever else makes you feel all warm and cozy. Since we are still obsessed with the lifestyle of the Scandinavians, people are now becoming obsessed with a new word: "lagom." When you try to translate this word into English, you get "not too much and not too little." It is the correct amount of anything you need. Basically, lagom is more able to balance and moderation.

There are many articles and books that are on the market about this subject that tells us ways we can live lagom. The Swedish people have always ranked as one of the top ten happiest countries in the entire world. Many people wonder if it could be their way of life that helps them achieve this. Do other people worry about lagom fizzling out in places where moderation has never been a concept before? People have always looked for more, more, more than being happy with what they already have.

· · ·

Just like hygge, lagom encompasses being grateful since it is all about being content in every season. Lagom isn't like hygge since it doesn't try to be indulgent or sexy. It can be easy to want one more cup of tea or coffee each morning or to have a nap at lunch; take the time to enjoy your favorite book. It isn't as appealing to think about getting rid of all the things you have too much of to be more lagom.

This could be the main reason why lagom isn't as popular as hygge. For all the articles that talk about its benefits, there are others that beg readers not to follow every Swedish footstep.

So, what could lagom offer to us when trying to live a life that is more balanced? Is this a good concept to try and teach our children?

Is It the Same As Minimalism

Some people have described lagom as living a minimalist lifestyle but in a bit of a different way. It doesn't matter if it is putting together a few articles of clothing to have the perfect wardrobe, stopping volunteering from working overtime, or figuring out how much to eat; lagom helps Swedes make decisions, so they are always on the right side of moderation.

It isn't a bad idea to try and teach our children about moderation as a way to guide them. Most countries raise their children to live in constant excess, and as parents, we worry about our children growing up thinking just about themselves and not worrying about anyone else. Lagom helps you focus on the whole and about just taking your portion and nobody else's. This is both considerate and wise. There is a lot of interest in living a minimalist life and being more simplistic in the United States, and this shows that right now might be the right time to introduce lagom to your house.

Lagom also has a great impact on the environment. Since you will be buying less, you won't have as much waste, and you will be using only what you have. This is an excellent way to live sustainably and have a lagom life. Just buying what you actually need, buying from local sources, and growing your own food can help teach our children that we can live with less and still be happy.

Creating an attitude of moderation can be brought into your relationships, too. Just think about the way Swedish people interact with one another. This is when all the questions about the benefits of this lifestyle start being asked.

Adjusting to the concept of lagom is not going to be simple or easy. Most people aren't ready for how lagom can make Americans think that Swedish people are cold and distant. All the boasting and gregariousness of the American lifestyle have to be done away with, and that can leave a lot of quietnesses. It is going to take some time for you to understand this is just another side effect of how lagom works with relationships.

Other people aren't too nice when they talk about lagom and social situations. Richard Orange wrote an article about this new concept, and he named it "his adopted country's suffocating doctrine of Lutheran self-denial." He says that lagom means you have to "be moderate in politics, views, and personality," anyone who lives outside of this norm or who lives a life that is passionate feels ostracized from the people who practice this way of living.

Relational Lagom and Its Benefits

You are going to have some landmines that you need to watch out for when you are trying to put lagom in your social interactions and relationships. Nevertheless, it can still give you some benefits. Lagom gets rid of boasting behaviors and comparisons. It is the total opposite of trying to "keep up with the Joneses. It turns the focus to make sure we don't take anything of the Joneses, whether it is something they own or their time.

With some time, you are going to become more comfortable with the silence that comes once everybody stops bragging about what they have and everything they have done. It will soon feel liberating when you don't have to wear everything you have accomplished on your sleeve.

It is a type of confidence you should want for your children and yourself. This is the "be proud of yourself and doesn't constantly seek outside approval" confidence everyone needs to have. You won't be trying to be liked or loved for what you have or the things you can do. Living the lagom lifestyle means you aren't teaching your children that bragging all the time, doing more, or having everything is what makes them feel loved and special.

The Perfect Amount of Lagom

The main thing to remember when trying to have a successful lagom might be just applying it in a "lagom-like" manner. The author of *Live Lagom: Balanced Living, The Swedish Way*, Anna Brones, states that her mother is Swedish, and she moved to the US to try to get away from lagom. She said it wasn't at all about "less balance but more about being the social equalizer, the things that restrained you and kept you from being who you really wanted to be and being able to express who you really are." Since her mom was an artist, lagom, to her, was very confining.

But lagom still managed to creep its way into her family life in how they ate, how they interacted with nature and the things they bought. Her mom actually lived lagom in several ways without even noticing it, and it soon became the norm in their home, and they learned to appreciate it.

The secret to living lagom is how you define what is optimal to you. It has to be used once the time is right and how it works best for you. Nobody else's personal lagom will ever be the same as yours. Just like everyone's DNA is different, their lagom will be too.

Everyone has to make their own decisions about lagom and what is right for every situation and when it isn't, along with what "just right" means to you. This can help make the lagom experience more of a guide rather than a straightjacket that confines your every move.

If moderation and balance are the goals of lagom, it has a lot to offer us. You can apply it to the way you engage with work, alcohol consumption, food consumption, technology, along a lot of other things. In lagom's best form, it can be the magic of "good enough" that knocks out our compulsion to be satisfied with everything, to do more, and to work harder in all areas of our lives.

Why Children Need Lagom

There isn't any question that kids nowadays are a lot different from the world Generation X grew up in. We live in a place where children can have anything they want when they want it. You might not want to believe it, but science shows us that this can cause a very unhealthy lifestyle, stress, and anxiety. This can have the same effects on children, too.

Everybody has walked into a toy store, and you get smacked in the face with aisles upon aisles of all sorts of toys that are going to make their way into a landfill once a child has played with them a few times. The normal American house is full of these over-stimulating, singing, and light-up toys that don't bring any value to a child. But when you use the lagom philosophy on your child's toys, it will let your child use their creativity and imagination to the max.

The Swedish concept of lagom is a way to live more content, less complicated, fairer, and simpler life. This lifestyle can be wonderful for a child. The lagom philosophy gives us a great guide when picking out toys for our children. You need to look for toys that are made from sustainable materials rather than just choosing the newest trending toys. Try your best to find timeless toys that your child can enjoy for years to come and maybe even hand down to their children. Keep reading to find the many benefits of lagom on children.

- Helps A Child's Imagination

The lagom lifestyle encourages a child to allow their imagination run wild. Since they won't have as many toys or video games, all the things in their room lets them have more creative and independent play. Children have an innate ability of creating imaginative scenarios totally by themselves without a bunch of toys. You won't believe the kind of play that a simple teddy bear can create. Give them some hand puppets and be ready for a show.

- Better Social Skills

Since your child has less toys, there will be more opportunities for better communications and sharing. If a child isn't distracted by technology, they will actually enjoy working out their social interactions with friends.

- Stress Levels Will Be Lower

Having too many toys can make for a very cluttered room and everyone knows that organizing and cleaning a room can cause a lot of stress if you don't have to space to keep things clean. If the child has lots of bins, toy boxes, and shelves to keep their toys in and on, it can lower their stress and anxiety.

What to Look For to Find Lagom Toys

- Won't Over-Entertain

If you find a toy that moves, sings, or lights up, it is a toy that you should not bring into your home. Most toys that make sounds can over-stimulate your child, so you can just imagine what a child is going through when they have a room full of toys that make sounds.

- Grows With The Child

Try to choose a toy that grows with your child. This is going to save you money, but it can slow down the cycle of toys being thrown away.

- Stirs Their Imagination

A simple fabric doll can give a child hours of entertainment. I remember as a child, putting my stuffed animals and dolls around me on the sofa and reading to them. My mom has pictures of this, and I believe this was when I developed my love of books. I would pretend to feed them, I took them outside to play, and would put them to bed for a nap. Even though most people look at stuffed animals and dolls as simple toys, it gives a child the ability to grow their imagination and creativity while playing.

- Helps Exploratory Play

This is basically any play time that lets a child use their senses while learning about their world. It helps their curiosity grow and lets them look at abstract concepts in the great big world around them.

- Can Be Used More Than Once

Wooden blocks are a wonderful toy because a child can use them in many different ways. A child can build tall towers, which helps build their fine and gross motor skills. If you buy blocks that have pictures, numbers, and letters on them, you can teach them about animals, colors, counting, and their letters.

three
food and lagom

THE DANES MAY BE big on cozy comfort food when it comes to hygge, but the Swedes have their own unique take on food with lagom. With food, lagom represents the never-too-extreme approach to eating and dieting. The Nordic diet is known for a healthy mixture of vegetables, fish, and whole grains with a midday coffee and sweet break known as "Fika." While the majority of the world likes to swing from over-the-top food trends and cleanses, the Swedes like to keep things simple by sticking to lagom.

The Swedes have managed to find a balance in their diet that the rest of the world hasn't. For example, if you were to ever go into a pizzeria in Sweden, you are probably going to encounter a crunchy slaw side dish that goes with every order. They call it a pizzasallad. It's just a simple slaw that has a vinegary dressing.

Another great example of the lagom way of food is the Swedes preferred type of milk. They don't drink whole milk, which would be too fatty. They also don't drink skim, which wouldn't be fatty enough. Instead, they consume something in between,

1.5% milk. They call it mellanmjolk, which they like to mix into their medium-brew coffee.

What does a lagom-oriented diet look like? For one, not eating an entire pint of ice cream in a single sitting. Also, embrace simple, modest foods, such as roast chicken, buttered multigrain toast, and soft-boiled eggs. They are also big on cooking wasteless and without a bunch of meat as this emphasizes the importance of sustainability that lagom is all about. You can also enjoy chili and even a potluck where there is just enough food for everybody to eat. Lagom is all about everything in moderation.

Fika

I've mentioned fika a few times in this book, so let's take a moment to look at what it is since we are talking about food. Fika is a traditional coffee break. Now, we are all probably familiar with the idea of a coffee break, but fika isn't quite the same. Fika serves as a chance for people to slow down and enjoy life.

The big distinguishing factor between fika and a regular coffee break, and is likely what makes people fall in love with it, is that it's about slowing down. For the Swedes, coffee represents a true break. It serves as a moment to sit and contemplate things on your own or with others. In the American culture, coffee is more about grabbing a 16-ounce-grande-whatever and getting on the road. It's about being as fast as possible. In Sweden, you look forward to the coffee. It's a moment where everything stops, and you give to just live in the moment. In our crazy world, we all crave the chance to get to slow down.

. . .

There are a number of different recipes for treats that are traditionally eaten during fika, but the great thing is, there is no fika police. The only thing that is required is brewing a cup of coffee or tea if that's more your thing, eating something delicious, and taking a break.

In Sweden, they make sure to incorporate fika into their everyday life in various ways. At offices in Sweden, they always have a fika break in the morning and afternoon. Fika serves as an excuse for friends to meet up and spend some quality time with each other. If you have to take a train to a place, you will pack a thermos of coffee and some baked goods, and if you didn't have the time to take something with you, there would likely be a fika special on the train. These normally include a cup of coffee with some type of sweet bun. Fika serves as a lifestyle and not just a simple coffee break.

Fika, after all, is about embracing the slow life, especially if you plan on making classic fika treats by scratch.

Swedish Breakfast

American breakfast goes big. We've got Egg McMuffins, breakfast burritos, Grand Slams, and Cronuts. No matter where you are in the world, you can likely ask for an all-American breakfast and be given orange juice, toast, bacon, and eggs. While there is nothing inherently wrong with our traditional breakfast, you can sometimes yearn for something just a bit less showy. The Swedish people can give us just that.

Swedes very rarely eat out for breakfast. Instead, they like to have quiet mornings at home, which can be quite the culture shock for people in America, especially those in big cities with a diner on every corner.

While porridge or oatmeal has been the historical breakfast of everybody, there are a number of other traditions that are deeply ingrained in Swedish foods. One of the most basic staples is what is known as filmjölk, or soured buttermilk. The Swedes like to flavor filmjölk with raspberry or vanilla, and then they will pour it over a bowl of muesli or cereal. It is tart, tangy, and adds a new flavor dimension.

Then they have what is called knäckerbröd, or crisp bread. This has been the heart of Swedish cuisine for over 500 years. If stored properly, this simple bread made from rye flour could last a year. While it is bland and cardboard-like in texture, it isn't meant to be eaten plain. Swedes will put a number of different foods on top of the bread, including cucumbers, peppers, cheese, butter, boiled eggs, and caviar.

Also, the Swedes are a big fan of strong coffee. In fact, Swedes drink more coffee per capita than everywhere else except for the Netherlands and Finland. It makes sense, too. They have a social life that is built around coffee, and when it comes to those dark, long winters, that third or fourth cup sounds great.

They also aren't fans of having pastries for breakfast. While there are no pastries to be had at breakfast, they do have fika, which is kind of like a second breakfast, where pastries are common. Also, that famous Swedish pancake is a no-frills, crepe-like sheet of batter and is served more like a lunch item and often comes with pea soup

Historical Traditions That Last

Before the Agricultural Revolution, Swedes would have to depend on what was locally available. Where a person lived would dictate which grains, vegetables, and meats could be consumed. This is why moose and reindeer are popular protein sources for the Arctic Sami (indigenous people of the upper north parts of the country), and the southern Vikings would rely on smaller games like wild boar and grouse.

Sweden has been practicing food preservation methods since early Viking times. Richer people would use methods like smoking and salting, while those who weren't as well off would choose to pickle, dry, or ferment their produce and fish. Fermented and pickled foods have stayed a big part of the Swedish diet, and popular types are cabbage, cucumbers, and other vegetables. Pickled herring is also a big part of holidays like Christmas, Easter, and Midsummer.

The preservation of food started to change in the mid-1800s with the Agricultural Industrialization. Being able to mechanize crop production, movement, and storage caused the food culture to shift from seasonal practices into regional traditions. Farms became more consolidated, and now technologies were introduced. Families began the move into major cities. Their products become mixed with imported raw goods, or they weren't produced in the country at all.

The invention of the wood-burning stove revolutionized how they ate even more by giving them the chance to stew, fry, or roast whatever they wanted. Previously, nearly all of their foods would be boiled. In fact, a lot of their most common foods started to take shape during the late 19th and 20th centuries.

For more than a millennium, bread and porridge have been staples in the Swedish kitchen. The population would rely on water mills that would only turn twice a year, and their bread would have to last longer periods of time. This is why they created their crisp bread that would last until they could make more. In the South, where they had windmills, they could bake bread more often, which meant southerners could have softer bread.

Popular protein sources from back in the day were fish, pork, cheese, milk, and elk. In the northern part of Sweden, reindeer was, and still is, a big part of Sami culture. The most popular vegetables that they grew in the past were rutabagas, turnips, and onions. Root vegetables grew wells in this climate, and they were also kept for a very long time. Around 1720, the Swedish culinary world saw the potato, which slowly started to replace root vegetables as the most important basc produce. It has continued to be a big part of the Swedish diet.

Humanskost is still a big part of Swedish culture, which translates to comfort food. This often consists of hearty meals that consist of potato, meat, and a boiled vegetable. Some classics in Sweden are smoked pork sausages served with creamed dill potatoes, yellow pea soup served with pancakes, and root vegetable mash and pork sausage.

International Influences

Local produce is a big part of Swedish food culture, but there are a number of classic dishes that have international roots. This is due to the fact that Swedes like to explore and try new dishes and flavors, and they incorporate them with their local ingredients. This creates some amazing dishes.

During the early 17th century, the influence of France started to make its way into Swedish cuisine. This created the creamy, rich sauces that Swedes still love. One of the most well known national dishes is meatballs, which was brought by King Charles XII from Turkey during the 18th century. The Swedes made this meal their own by complementing the meatballs with some local favorites like lingonberries, pickled cucumber, and potatoes, and they would smother the meatballs with a creamy gravy. This is what has become known as Swedish meatballs around the world.

There are also other global specialties, like Turkish kebabs and lasagna, that have become a part of Swedish cuisine. Pizza that is topped with béarnaise sauce and beef filets and kebab pizza are national favorites that mix a culture clash of ingredients to make something that is completely Swedish. On Fridays, it's common for families to enjoy tacos. These are inspired by Mexican traditions, but the Swedish people have made them their own.

With their large history of trading, exotic spices like saffron, anise, cardamom, and cinnamon have become a part of their baked goods.

· · ·

Today, Swedes are big on eating as naturally as they can to ensure they improve their health and the health of the planet. Animal welfare and food production ethics are of extreme importance for them. This is why they demand locally made, and organic products and a lot of the supermarkets will stock products that are created at local farms.

Sweden is big on the farm-to-table movement, and given the fact that they like to use their natural pantry of edible plants, mushrooms, and berries, you could go so far as to call it forest-to-table. A restaurant in Halland called Restaurant Ang by Astad Vineyard is the epitome of this. Their dishes are prepared with ingredients that they source from nearby farms, forests, lakes, and meadows.

Zero Waste

With the growing climate crisis, a lot of people are looking to find more sustainable dietary habits that have zero waste. Sweden is very big on this. Gram in Malmo became the first package-free grocery store. People would take their own containers and fill them up with the products they wanted.

In Stockholm, Paul Svensson, a chef, had led the charge to make a more sustainable restaurant culture. He owns the restaurant Fotografiska, which has a menu of plant-based items that make use of seasonal produce. They also have an option to add a meat-based side. They grind up mussel shells to make plates, and they use old wine bottles to make vases and glasses. They compost organic waste or use it as part of signature dishes.

· · ·

This isn't a new philosophy for them. Pyttipanna, a Swedish classic, is a one-skillet dish that uses leftovers like onion, potato, meat, and whatever else a person could find in their fridge.

A big part of Sweden's food culture uses everything that their country can offer. They mix local produce with various international influences to make dishes that have evolved and adapted along with its culture. Sustainability and innovation have stayed a huge driving force in their food scene.

Traditional Dishes and Food

One popular dish is called gravadlax and is made by curing salmon in a solution of sugar, dill, and salt. Traditionally, the Nordic fishermen would place fish underground to ferment it, which is why this meal was given the name grava, which translates to dig.

In Sweden, you can find this dish thinly sliced and served with a mustard sauce. They also serve it with pickled herring and are often a centerpiece of every smorgasbord.

Lingonberry jam is very popular in Sweden and accompanies a number of their dishes, from black pudding and meatballs to porridge and pancakes. Lingonberry is very similar in taste to cranberries, but they are a bit sweeter and aren't as tart as cranberry.

Ärtsoppa is a popular golden soup that they make from ham, root vegetables, and dried peas, along with other spices. It is a traditional home-cooked meal and has been around since the 13th century. They most commonly have it on Thursdays, and it is served with cream, jam, and pancakes. It is believed that this dish was popularized during the Middle Ages when the Swedes would follow along with the Christian tradition of meat fasting on Fridays.

A popular potato pancake is called raggmunk and is more commonly seen during the winter months. They top these pancakes with sweetened lingonberries and salted pork.

Then there is the Rårakor, which is the smaller cousin of the raggmunk. It is a potato fritter that they serve with savory toppings such as chives, onions, crème Fraiche, and caviar.

In August and September, the Swedish people have a kräftskiva, which is a crayfish party. These are outdoor parties where you get all-you-can-peel-and-eat fish along with drinking songs and aquavit.

I've mentioned how the Sami people like reindeer. One of the most popular dishes they make with meat is called renskav. It is a winter favorite among them. It is made with frozen reindeer meat that has been buried. They shave the meat as needed and fry it up with mushrooms. A more modern version uses potatoes, onions, cream, and lingonberries.

A popular Swedish delicacy is called Surströmming, which is known for its pungent smell. It is made from a Baltic herring that has fermented so much that it is pretty much rotten. Given the fact of how it smells, there is one right way and several wrong ways to open up the can. Swedes will not eat the fish right out of the can. They will fillet it and then wrap it up in some buttered flatbread. They top it with crème Fraiche, diced onion, and almond potatoes.

Swedish Traditions

There are a number of other traditions that Swedes have that center around food, family, and friends. Let's take a look at other traditions that can help you live a more lagom life.

- Fredags mys

Fredags Mys, meaning Friday cozy, is a popular concept in Sweden. What is it? Well, it's all about eating comfort foods, which normally consist of pizza and tacos, or you share snacks with your family. It's a very easy tradition to adopt.

- Lördags godis

The normal Swedish family will have two children and two adults. They eat about 1.2 kilos of sweets every week. Most of this is eaten on sweets day or Saturday. This is done to protect their teeth and to keep cavities away. This tradition has been historically linked to some questionable medical practices.

During the 40s and 50s, an experiment that was debated at the time involved sweets. It was done at Vipeholm Mental Hospital located in Lund. The staff fed patients huge amounts of sweets to try and cause tooth decay. This was just one of many experiments done on humans, all in the name of research. This was based on some findings done in 1957 about the relationship between tooth decay and sweets. Their medical board said that Swedes should eat sweets only one day a week. That was one unwritten rule that most families still partake of.

Sweden was able to achieve its goal for improved dental health decades ago by implanting this. They only have candy on Saturdays. Apparently, it is healthier on your teeth if you consume all of your gummy bears on a single say. Having a binge candy day that also means better dental health? That is something I think we can all get on board with.

- Last Piece

This is a quintessential Swedish practice where you make just a little bit more of whatever you are cooking. It isn't so much to do with being wasteful than it is about being polite. A host never wants to offer a person too little, and the guest understands this. Svenska biten, as they sometimes call it, is a reciprocal act of being polite.

- Calendar of Sweets

If you visit Sweden, you will always be able to find a good excuse to eat something sweet. This is such a tradition that certain calendar days have been set aside to celebrate a specific sugary confection. October 4th is cinnamon bun day for example.

Buns called semlor are filled with almond paste, and cream gets eaten on fat Tuesday or Shrove Tuesday, as the Swedes know it. This is the day before Ash Wednesday or the first day of Lent.

. . .

March 25th is the day for waffles. November 6th, they eat a
sponge cake that is decorated with either marzipan silhouettes in
the shape of King Gustav II Adolf or chocolate. This is in honor
of the monarch who was killed at the Battle of Lutzen in 1632

- Singing for Dinner

The Swedes love to celebrate things, and they even have national
holidays for all of their favorite foods. What might not be as well
known is that they have a tradition of singing at the dinner table.
This is even common in student unions, and a number of families also pick up their glasses for a cheer and song during festive
dinners like Christmas, Easter, New Year's, and Midsummer.

- Lingonberries

Just like mustard and ketchup are staples in American foods,
lingonberry jam is used in various dishes like black pudding,
porridge, pancakes, and meatballs. Even though it is sweet, they
very seldom use it on bread. Because they have the "right of
public access," everybody can go wherever they want to on public
land, and they pick lingonberries whenever they want. They use
the tiny red fruit to make a preserve that is similar to jam.

- Pickled Herring

You could swap out meatballs or choose a cured salmon over a
smoked one or choose mini sausages, but a smorgasbord isn't
going to be complete without some pickled herring on it. This
favorite is still the basis of every buffet in Sweden.

. . .

Because there is such an abundance of herring in the Baltic and North Seas, the Swedes have been pickling this fish since the Middle Ages, mostly as a way to preserve fish so it can be easily transported and stored. You can find pickled herring in various flavors like dill, garlic, onion, and mustard. It is normally eaten with sharp hard cheese, chopped chives, sour cream, potatoes, boiled eggs, and crispbread.

- Räksmörgås

Anytime you order a sandwich in Sweden, don't get surprised if you get one slice of bread. This is the normal Swedish smörgås. They had eaten open sandwiches since the 1400s, when huge slabs of bread were used as their plates.

The shrimp sandwich is still the option that is fed to kings. This sandwich is piled with sliced boiled eggs, cucumber, tomato, and lettuce. It is usually topped with some creamy romsas or crème Fraiche that has been blended with roe and sprigs of dill. These sandwiches are an integral part of their culture. Their saying of "gilda in pa en rakmacka" or translated to "glide in on a shrimp sandwich." It actually corresponds to an expression called "get a free ride," which means to have an advantage without doing anything to deserve it.

- Crispbread

Other than just having bread and butter, crispbread is always served with the main meal. This is what most Swedes will automatically reach for when they sit down at a table. It was at one time thought to be "poor man's food," it has been baked for more than 500 years. As mentioned previously, it can last an entire year if you store it the right way. The remnants are the most edible and versatile part.

During the 1970s, the "Swedish National Board of Health and Welfare" suggested that they need to eat between six and eight slices of bread daily. Crispbread can come in different flavors, thicknesses, and shapes. Go into any store in Sweden, and you will find shelves covered with it. You can top crispbread with things like caviar that gets squeezed out of a tube or boiled egg slices for breakfast. For lunch, top it with some sliced cucumber, cheese, and ham. You can butter some sliced crispbread to have with your evening meal.

- Pancakes and Pea Soup

Most Swedes grew up eating pancakes and pea soup on Thursdays. This tradition is still being done by the "Swedish Armed Forces." They have been doing this since World War II. Even though its real origins have been debated, from the Catholics not being able to eat meat on Friday and eating their fill on pea soup on Thursday to pea soup being so easy to make by maids who would only work for half a day on Thursdays, this tradition has stuck. Many lunch restaurants will still serve pancakes with lingonberry jam and pea soup every Thursday.

- Prinsesstårta

This is known as a princess cake. This delicacy will color the windows in bakeries all over Sweden and is a favorite that has been around since the 1920s. This cake is made from layers of yellow cake that have been lined with vanilla custard and jam. It gets finished off with some whipped cream. The cake is then topped with a bright pink sugar rose. It is carefully sealed with a thin layer of green marzipan.

This cake debuted during the 1920s due to Jenny Akerstrom. She taught Princesses Astrid, Martha, and Margaretha. These were the daughters of Prince Carl Bernadotte. These little princesses loved the cake so much that the cake was named after them.

The third week in September is known as princess cake week, but this delicacy is eaten during festivals and has been used to mark several milestones in their daily lives. Now, it can be bought in many colors, from the normal green to red during Christmas, orange during Halloween, white at weddings, and yellow for Easter.

- Surströmming

You aren't going to find a culture that doesn't have at least one culinary delight that makes visitors and locals cringe. During the late part of August until the early part of September, this stinky tradition is done in Sweden, especially in the north. During this time, cans upon cans of sour fermented Baltic herring are opened and eaten, well by many, not all. This tradition has been done since the 1700s. The cans are opened outside because of the unpleasant, overpowering smell that many have compared to raw sewage and rotten eggs. This tradition is done on the third Thursday in August each year.

four
making your style lagom

THE NEWEST SCANDINAVIAN trend called lagom can upgrade your closet in no time. Ellos, the Swedish plus-sized brand, was the first to introduce people to lagom. Lagom simply means "not too much, not too little, just right." This is the way the Swedes tap into their coveted but almost never reached balance in life. It is the perspective that most people are looking for to help give their closet an overhaul.

We all want to find our happy medium in life. The message lagom wants to give you is that you need to find peace in all the simple things in life. Most people try to get through their lives by maximizing their schedules and beating deadlines. They have forgotten how to stay grounded and centered. People now live lives that are full. At Ellos, they have created "National Lagom Day" to help their employees remember to remain balanced and peaceful in their lives.

It would be safe to say that Ellos is finally doing the right things. They have a label that is affordable, and they carry sizes from ten all the way to 34. They have been popular in Scandinavia since they were first founded in 1947. I had the chance to go to Stockholm to see more about this lagom idea. Between bike rides in nature and fikas (that wonderful Swedish coffee break), I was able to center myself and unplug from the world around me. That was so not what I was used to in my daily life. I was able to grab some pointers on ways to use lagom in my closet. Keep reading to find a few ways you too can lagom your closet.

How to Lagom the Latest Trends

Most people don't try all the latest trends they see in magazines or on social media, but it is fun trying some of them. Using lagom to approach the newest trends is more about being selective with the looks that you decide to try. Keep in mind "not too much, not too little." A simple tip to help you master your lagom look is to try a new print or color like an animal, neon, or metallic. Add in a classic silhouette such as a sleek coat, a wrap-around dress, or a blazer. These familiar but simple shapes will offset any bold embellishments.

Staying Within Your Budget

Most of the time, fashion gets defined by extremes. On one end, you will have cult powerhouses making insanely cheap clothing, while on the other end, you have the luxury brands that cost you thousands of dollars for one item. How can lagom help you stay within your budget?

The main thing you have to remember is moderation. Find some articles that are very well made that make you happy but are still within your budget. This is going to be very different for everybody since it is based on your income. It would be safe to say that a $15 jacket won't be a good investment for a wardrobe if you want it to last you a long time. But on the other hand, spending

$800 on a jacket won't make you happy if you have to go weeks without paying your bills or eating. Remember, lagom is all about staying balanced.

Decluttering Your Closet With Lagom

People who claim to be expert shoppers are going to buy pieces that begin collecting dust hanging in their closets. Don't worry because there is a lagom solution. A lagom wardrobe is similar to a minimalist's wardrobe: it will be very practical, and you will have to get rid of any clothes that you haven't used or no longer want and replace them with a few very versatile garments that you love that can all be worn together.

The Ultimate Lagom Wardrobe

The lagom lifestyle went viral back in 2017, which is funny because being viral is so not lagom. Lagom helps you live a life full of balance and fairness. It isn't anything like its Danish neighbor hygge that is all about feelings. Lagon is more of a social code that is ever-present in the Swede's society. It helps with everything from conversations to making sure everyone knows that nobody takes the last cookie. When you decide to lagom your wardrobe, you won't just have a minimalist closet. It will be one of sustainability, comfort while allowing you to live a "buy less, buy better" philosophy.

- How Fashion Follows Lagom

Within the world of Swedish fashion, you can find all sorts of designs from exclusive to affordable from brands like Filippa K, Boomerang, COS, Rodebjer, Tiger of Sweden, Acne Studios,

WeSC, Weekday, and H&M. Mostly known for the furniture, interior pioneers at IKEA follow a fashion scene that is huge, especially since they cater to agender and unisex. The industry is also the "throw-away attitude" that most people love to resist. Many brands are introducing more organic and durable clothing options that allow their customers to purchase garments seen on catwalks.

H&M is normally dismissed with some criticism like the ones directed toward IKEA since 2011 because they use harmful chemicals in their products. They have been trying hard to reach zero pollutants being released into the atmosphere. By recycling and reusing, this brand hopes to turn into a totally circular enterprise.

The Swedish Fashion Council is taking more steps to keep industries sustainable by launching the "Swedish Fashion Ethical Charter." This covers the whole industry that includes designers, stylists, advertising agencies, and modeling. Theirs is a very unique initiative and tries to give guidelines to have a more sustainable industry.

- Sustainable Legacy

The modern designs in Sweden are lagom in many ways. It balances forward-thinking innovations with its proud heritage while putting sustainability and functionality first, no matter the price. Ingvar Kamprad, the founder of IKEA, said that it was food for thought. If quality and affordability are not mutually exclusive, maybe our "throw away culture" began as a way to have affordable products and not as a response to the low quality of products on the market. If you take care of your IKEA products, they could last your entire life.

- Comfy Chic Swedish Style

Since Sweden is a fashion nation, they are great at basic styles that are comfortable with various understated cuts and details. Their clothing was designed to let people run outside quickly, and they easily became experts at dressing practically. They stand out from the crowd in their lagom a bit but not too much. At home, most of the population is like a huge monochrome mass, but if you travel abroad, you can quickly spot a Swedish person in a huge crowd; their style of keeping fashion low-key seems too extravagant.

- Lagom on Fashion

Swedes don't use their clothing to display messages, patterns, or colors. They think this is a luxury that you should only see in the fashion industry. They aren't big on fashion houses. They focus more on frugality and functionalism. Clothes are thought of as consumables and items that are great to have. Clothes are for everybody and the things that everyone needs have to be lagom. They can't be too crazy or too colorful. Yes, it can get boring, but it can also be liberating. They dress for "casual Friday" each day, and everybody relaxes a lot more.

- Saving Is A Virtue

Swedes celebrate frugality daily. They love clothes that are affordable because they think it is vulgar to "splash out." There is a balance they have to find since their respect for things is linked to price. They will fix a broken zipper on an expensive coat than go out and buy another one. They can easily buy cheap clothing and replace things as they need to.

- Giving Your Wardrobe a Facelift

Since the fashion scene keeps moving, your style usually moves with it. How you look at the things in your closet might change some too. Look at what is in your closet regularly. You can't just focus on fashion trends. You might find a skirt you forgot you had and realize that it still works as a cute petticoat for another dress that needed a facelift. Take some snapshots of you wearing it, and then think about it for a day. This will help you think about what you found.

- Get Out The Sewing Machine

People have been throwing out their sewing machines and pianos. When we do that, we are throwing away our knowledge and skills. Everybody needs to know how to sew on a button and change out a zipper and who knows, you might decide to upcycle an old garment into a brand new article of clothing. You can find all kinds of videos that show you how on YouTube.

- Take a Look at Your Minimalist Wardrobe

It is fine to have some basic clothes that you love wearing all the time. It might be time to move away from this idea of having a specific type of clothing for everybody. Your base might be ten-print dresses, but your friend needs a range of trousers and jackets.

- Learn How To "Ugly Match"

You might have heard the phrase "ugly matching." It can feel liberating to try something new, do it completely wrong, and then just live with it. You can't really find yourself or your true style until you experiment with different looks and you have learned to trust your instincts. You might just find that you love something that the fashion world thinks is ugly.

Ways to Be Functional

- Take Care Of Your Clothes

In order to survive in the cold and rain, you have to have some quality things, but in order to have quality, you might have to spend some money. When you look at buying an overcoat, think long-term. Whether you need to weatherize your winter boots each year or buy a new pair.

- Quit Worrying About Fads

When you can learn to think about more long-term needs, you quit thinking about all the fashion trends. You will be able to purchase clothes that you truly like. I'm not saying you can't be part of the fashion trend. Having colorful rain gear won't ever go out of style, and it still keeps you warm and dry.

- Make Sure It's Comfortable

Nothing is going to ruin your days like bleeding toes or heels. You have to purchase shoes that are very comfortable. You will be able to walk more, which is also lagom since you will be getting some exercise and fresh air.

Getting Into a Functional Mindset

You might have heard about an old Swedish proverb that says: "There is no bad weather, only bad clothes." They refer to this when talking to tourists about their super cold winters. Their attitude is very real. They have perfected living in sub-zero weather and extreme weather changes. Everybody knows that you can stay warm by wearing layers. Everybody knows that you put wool clothing closest to your skin. The lagom way to survive is by making your home cozy and stylish enough that you love staying inside, but you have to make sure your wardrobe is up for this challenge when you have to go face the harsh elements.

It took me a long time to not want to put a thermometer in my window when I moved to America. The Swedes have a different wardrobe for each season. They also have a storage system packed away in their attic so they can replace one season's box with the next one when it rolls around. Because of this, they don't look at any type of weather as being bad. Since they have a thermometer in their window, they know what clothes they need to put on each day.

five
lagom and the world

WE'RE ALL WELL aware of the global changes that are happening. With all of these changes, we have to find new ways to help preserve what we have left of the world and find new sustainable ways to make a difference. Lagom is a great tool to help do that. Since it's all about taking just what you need, it reduces the amount of waste and unused products.

Lagom aims to help you create a happier, better, and more balanced way of living. It's about living in a sustainable manner by saving water and energy and creating less waste, and recycling more.

This can be seen in a number of businesses that have chosen to put lagom at the forefront of the business.

The first company we are going to look at is IKEA. IKEA is a Swedish home furnishing store, and they have created a line of products known as the Live Lagom project. It has been about a seven-year behavior change initiative that looked to see how to do better than the conventional approaches businesses took and how they could support more sustainable development by helping customers to live sustainable lives.

Thanks to IKEA, they have made it easier for people to live a lagom life and a more sustainable life. Here are just a few ways that their products can help people live a more sustainable life.

- Save Energy

IKEA is serious about helping its consumers cut their energy consumption. They have a large range of LED lighting and solar-powered solutions. Not to mention the fact that they have energy-saving appliances like refrigerators, washing machines, and induction hobs. These all mean that you can keep costs down and help to reduce your impact on the world.

- Save Water

The people who have joined the live lagom project have become lovingly known as lagomers. As for their lagomers, they have found a number of ways to use less water by making tiny adjustments to things they do every day, from washing their hands to brushing their teeth. Their shower products are energy-efficient, which can help you to save up to 30% more water, and there isn't a difference in pressure.

- Waste Recycling

It is easy to reduce how much waste you produce, and that effort can have a huge impact on the world. IKEA has customized recycling solutions that can help any home and life through the use of sorting bins in their SORTERA and PLUGGIS ranges. It gives you the ability to recycle and get organized without a bunch of effort.

- Healthy Living

Eating good foods will not only have a good impact on your body and mind, but it can also improve the environment as well. Going with sustainably sourced meats and picking out more plant-based foods will help the planet because these types of foods don't take as many resources to make, and they have a much smaller carbon footprint.

Since 2014, IKEA has helped to create a sweeping movement of sustainable living as they have brought more people into the world of lagom. IKEA defines its lagomers as "A person who is working towards living a more lagom lifestyle – making small changes to their everyday life to minimize environmental impact, being thrifty with resources and enjoying a fun, happy and balanced life."

There isn't just one single way for a person to live a sustainable life. We all have to find a balance that works for us, but with shoe-string budgets and busy lives, it can get difficult when it comes to figuring out the best place to start.

Thanks to IKEA, and a number of other businesses, getting started is easier and more cost-efficient than ever before. The following are some easy steps to take to live a more sustainable life.

- Switch to LED

You can use very little energy when it comes to lighting your home by using LED bulbs that will last years longer than traditional light bulbs. LEDs used 85% less energy than incandescent, and in the spirit of their Live Lagom Project, IKEA has switched their entire lighting range to affordable and efficient LED lights.

- Switch off The Lights

This one is pretty easy. Switch off your bedroom light if you aren't currently in your bedroom, and make it a habitual thing whenever you leave a room in your house. The Energy Saving Trust has said that turning your lights off for just a few seconds can help to save more energy than it takes for the light to turn back on.

If you need to have some light for smaller spaces like wardrobes and cupboards, purchase motion sensors that will switch on when it detects movement, or if it's touched, and will switch off after 30 seconds.

- Use Rechargeable Batteries

You can save yourself a bunch of time by purchasing some rechargeable batteries. You can get a bunch more power out of your battery-operated appliances. It not only produces less waste, but it will also help you to save money.

- Switch Off Appliances

Whether it's your broadband modem, stereo, or TV, you should switch them off instead of letting them stay on standby when leaving your home. The Energy Saving Trust says that a household can save an average of $30 a year by doing this. This can be easier by plugging appliances into an extension cord, then all you have to do is unplug the main cord.

- Purchase Things Made from Bamboo

Bamboo is a renewable material that naturally grows fast and strong without the use of chemicals or irrigation. It is the best type of material to make plant pots, baskets, and bowls, so try to find bamboo products for these types of things.

- Take Shorter Showers

A typical bath will usually use 80 liters of water while taking a short shower can use a third of that. If everybody within the UK started taking a three-minute shower, they could save enough water equivalent to supplying a million homes each day. Setting a timer for your shower is the best way to accomplish this.

- Use your Washing to Its Fullest Capacity

Make the most out of every load of laundry you do by filling your washing machine to its fullest capacity. It's also just as effective to wash your clothes in cool water. Washing clothes in cool water instead of hot helps to save energy as well.

- Don't Always Tumble Dry

Tumble dryers cost a fortune to use, not to mention to buy, so why not let your clothes air dry when you can? Clothes can be air-dried inside or outside by using clotheslines or racks. Home-ware stores have a bunch of different types of drying racks that are also foldable, which helps to save space when you aren't using them.

- Control Overnight Heating

Turning your thermostat down a degree can help to cut your heating bill by ten percent. If you are afraid of getting cold at night, especially during the winter, you can add a thicker duvet or more blankets to your bed.

Duvets have a warmth scale known as a tog rating. A tog measurement lets you know how warm you will be if you sleep under a certain duvet. The tog measurement is found by looking at the materials' thermal insulation properties. When you are shopping for a new duvet, take a look at the tog rating. The lower the rating, the less warm the duvet will be. A duvet with a tog rating of 4.5 would be good for the summer months, and for the winter, a tog rating of 15 would be ultra-cozy.

- Draft-Proof your Home

Doing a little DIY in your home, especially at the start of the winter season, can help you draft-proof your home. Try tackling the doors and windows, and then block cracks in the floors. Rugs can also serve as a quick fix for bare floors so that you don't lose heat.

- Purchase an Induction Hob

You can bring energy efficiency into your kitchen by using induction hobs. They transfer energy directly into the pan so that there is a very minimal amount of heat wasted, and it provides you with an economical and quick way to cook. You can boil two liters of water in only five minutes, compared to the ten minutes it takes on a glass-ceramic hob. Also, if you're in the market for new pots and pans, go with cast iron or stainless steel. They are durable, and absorb heat well, retains it for longer, and spreads out the energy.

- Make The Most Out of Your Stovetop

You can multitask while saving energy and water by cooking your entire meal using one stove eye. IKEA has Stabil pan inserts that give you the ability to steam vegetables on top of boiling pasta.

- Lower Your Water Waste

Getting ready to wash dishes? Keeping your faucet running can waste a lot of water, but this can be reduced significantly by placing a bowl in the sink, filling it up, and using that to wash your dishes.

- Use a Dishwasher

Using a dishwasher not only saves you time and energy, but they tend to be more hygienic and energy-efficient than hand washing.

You should also ensure you use the eco-cycle option whenever you can.

- Organize Your Fridge

You can organize your fridge by using clear containers to help stack food up so that you can more easily see the things you have. Before you head out for a shopping trip, take a picture of what you have in your fridge so that you know exactly what it is that you need.

- Don't Waste food

If you plan out your meals for the week, it can help reduce the chance that you will overcook. Also, don't keep your foods out of sight; you should use clear food containers so that you can easily see what you have. You should also avoid rushing out to the store to purchase new foods. Make do with what you have on hand first.

- Reuse

Whether it's canvas shopping bags or travel mugs, reuse them over and over instead of wasting your money on disposable options.

- Learn How to Upcycle

Toilet paper rolls, cans, jars, yogurt tubs, cardboard, fabric, and paper; don't throw these things away. Instead, save them for your craft projects. If you have furniture that you don't need, you can try to adapt it into something that you can use. Don't put a limit on your creativity.

- Get Used to Recycling

Recycling a single aluminum can helps to save enough energy to help power a television for three hours. Come up with a recycling system that you can stick to for materials like metal, plastic, paper, and glass. Make sure your entire family joins in on this as well.

- Grow Food

Old containers make great mini gardens. Try growing your own food by planting herbs. This is cheaper and will give you fresh herbs all year long.

- Purchase Acacia Wood

When it comes to storage and furniture, try purchasing acacia wood. Acacia wood is known for its durability and strength, so it is a great material to use for outdoor furniture because it is weather-resistant and durable.

- Bring the Outside in Through a Vertical Garden

You can easily bring a touch of the outside indoor, and green up your home, but using a vertical garden. Hanging planters are a great way to do this.

- Try Using Solar Panels

For the majority of households, energy is one of the biggest expenses. A great way to reduce your energy bill is to install solar panels. IKEA has a pay-as-you-save SolarLoan scheme, and they have said "We're making it more affordable for as many people as possible to generate their own solar power."

- Enjoy Healthier Meals

Now, I'm not telling you that you can never indulge in a treat, but becoming more aware of what you consume and where it came from can be very beneficial. Consume more nutritious and sustainable options when choosing what to eat. It is also a good idea to buy local food. Especially during the summer; you could head to your local farmers market to get locally grown produce.

- Lower your Carbon Footprint

If you are looking to get a new car, look for a more fuel-efficient model. Not only does this help to lower your carbon footprint, but it will also help you to save money. You could also ditch the car altogether if at all possible, and start biking to work. Try taking walks or bike rides on the weekend when you need to go somewhere.

- Save Water When Brushing Your Teeth

When you are shaving or brushing your teeth, switch the water off instead of letting it run the entire time. Keep a cup at the sink that you use to rinse your mouth out.

- Purchase Energy Efficient Appliances

Looking for a new washer, dryer, or fridge? Take a little extra time to research and find a more energy efficient option that can help to reduce energy consumption without sacrificing performance.

- Improve Your Work

You can improve your wellbeing and health at work or in your home office by ensuring that your day is more productive. You can do this by investing in a sit-to-stand desk. This gives you more freedom during the day so that you can sit or stand whenever you want.

These are just some great ways that use the lagom philosophy of 'use what you need' and can help you live a more sustainable life.

Barcelona and Lagom Living

In Barcelona, they have created Lagom Living to help make something more than co-living spaces. They want to create home environments that empowers and inspires the people who live there to be active participants and creators in their world.

Lagom Living aims to be an environmentally sustainable way of living that puts people in harmony with the environment. They also want to create homes that support the wellbeing for those who live there. A home where people can flourish physically, socially, and mentally. They want to create a community where the people their feel as though they belong.

. . .

They want to create a new lifestyle with co-living. They believe that people are looking for more than just an apartment. At Lagom Living, they want to help foster that new lifestyle. They want to create a new living experience that connects people with others on a similar journey.

So what is co-living? There are two definitions that Lagom Living likes to use. One is, "a shared housing designed to support a purpose-driven life." The second is, "a modern, urban lifestyle that values openness, sharing, and collaboration."

They are also very selective about the type of people who stay there. That way they ensure the people who are there are like-minded and can contribute to each other's lives in a meaningful way.

As you can see, lagom has done a lot for the world in inspiring businesses and people alike to adopt a more sustainable life. Remember the tips we went over earlier. It doesn't take a lot of effort to make small changes to help make the planet just a bit healthier and happier.

afterword

Thank you for making it through to the end of *The Lagom Book*, let's hope it was informative and able to provide you with all of the tools you need to achieve your goals whatever they may be.

The next step is to start adding the lagom practices you like into your life. Lagom is a fairly simple way of living. With a little work and some time, you can live a lagom life. While this is a simple practice, it can bring so much to your life because it will make you life that much easier and more enjoyable. You won't miss out on the small things anymore.

Finally, if you found this book useful in any way, a review is always appreciated!

Further Reading

Go check out my other books where I'm exploring life happiness and purpose in other countries:

The Hygge Book: Living a Happy Life the Danish way.

The Ikigai Book: Finding Happiness and Purpose the Japanese way.

Printed in Great Britain
by Amazon